NOËLLE JANACZEWSKA IS a playwright, poet, essayist, and the author of *The Book of Thistles* (UWA Publishing, 2017). Much of her work deals with history's gaps and silences, focussing on people, plants, creatures and events which have been overlooked or marginalised in official records. Noëlle's work has been produced, broadcast and published locally and internationally, and in 2014 she received a prestigious Windham Campbell Prize from Yale University for her body of work as a dramatist. In Australia her plays and audio scripts have won a Queensland Premier's Literary Award (*Mrs Petrov's Shoe*), the Playbox-Asialink Playwriting Competition and the Griffin Award (both for *Songket*) and eight AWGIE (Australian Writers' Guild) Awards—for community and youth theatre and for radio works across drama and nonfiction. Find out more about Noëlle's writing at noelle-janaczewska.com or check out her food blog eatthetable.com

Jane Phegan in the 2016 Siren Theatre Company production of Good with Maps *at Kings Cross Theatre, Sydney. (Photo: Lucy Parakhina)*

Good with Maps
and
Teacup in a Storm

NOËLLE JANACZEWSKA

CURRENCY PRESS
SYDNEY

CURRENCY PLAYS

First published in 2018
by Currency Press Pty Ltd,
PO Box 2287, Strawberry Hills, NSW, 2012, Australia
enquiries@currency.com.au
www.currency.com.au

Copyright: *Charting Life: Noëlle Janaczewska's* Good with Maps *and* Teacup in a Storm © Laura Ginters, 2018; *Good with Maps* © Noëlle Janaczewska, 2018; *Teacup in a Storm* © Noëlle Janaczewska, 2018.

COPYING FOR EDUCATIONAL PURPOSES

The Australian *Copyright Act 1968* (Act) allows a maximum of one chapter or 10% of this book, whichever is the greater, to be copied by any educational institution for its educational purposes provided that that educational institution (or the body that administers it) has given a remuneration notice to Copyright Agency (CA) under the Act.

For details of the CA licence for educational institutions contact CA, 11/66 Goulburn Street, Sydney, NSW, 2000; tel: within Australia 1800 066 844 toll free; outside Australia 61 2 9394 7600; fax: 61 2 9394 7601; email: info@copyright.com.au

COPYING FOR OTHER PURPOSES

Except as permitted under the Act, for example a fair dealing for the purposes of study, research, criticism or review, no part of this book may be reproduced, stored in a retrieval system, or transmitted in any form or by any means without prior written permission. All enquiries should be made to the publisher at the address above.

Any performance or public reading of *Good with Maps* or *Teacup in a Storm* is forbidden unless a licence has been received from the author or the author's agent. The purchase of this book in no way gives the purchaser the right to perform the plays in public, whether by means of a staged production or a reading. All applications for public performance should be addressed to Cameron's Management, 7th Floor, 61 Marlborough Street, Surry Hills NSW 2010, Australia; ph: +61 2 9319 7199; email: info@cameronsmanagement.com.au

Typeset by Dean Nottle for Currency Press.
Cover design by Alissa Dinallo.

 A catalogue record for this book is available from the National Library of Australia

Contents

Introduction
   Laura Ginters — vii

GOOD WITH MAPS — 1

TEACUP IN A STORM — 31

Currency Press acknowledges the Traditional Owners of the Country on which we live and work. We pay our respects to all Aboriginal and Torres Strait Islander Elders, past and present.

Jane Phegan in the 2016 Siren Theatre Company production of Good with Maps *at Kings Cross Theatre, Sydney. (Photo: Lucy Parakhina)*

Charting Life: Noëlle Janaczewska's *Good with Maps* and *Teacup in a Storm*

'Write what only you can write. Be adventurous. Court risk. Dare to be unfashionable.' – Noëlle Janaczewska[1]

Noëlle Janaczewka has certainly followed her own advice to writers. She has been described as 'one of contemporary Australia's most evocative playwrights',[2] and her skill and innovation in writing for performance (both theatre and radio) has been recognised in the multiple awards she has received in Australia, and internationally.[3] (She writes what only she can write.) It is ironic, then, that her work has been largely overlooked by mainstream theatre companies in Australia—although as she reflectively notes, 'their programming decisions are often quite conservative and I am not a conservative writer'.[4] The publication of these two recent plays, *Good with Maps* (2017) and *Teacup in a Storm* (2018), is a welcome move to make this work more accessible and widely known to theatre-makers, theatre-lovers, and indeed readers or writers with a passion for the expansive possibilities of the performative written form.

Court risk ...

A prolific and accomplished writer of plays, performance texts, lyrics and libretti, monologues, poetry, essays and radio scripts (both drama and non-fiction), Janaczewska's writing for performance is characterised by a sense of adventure, not only in her choice of theme and subject matter, but also for the form each work takes. She is, it seems, only constrained by a disdain for the tired conventions of mainstage naturalism. (This is succinctly and pointedly indicated in her Production Notes for *Good with Maps*, for example, where she stipulates: 'its staging requirements are basic—but absolutely no sofas'.[5]) Just as she has always vigorously rejected delimiting labels for herself (such as 'girl director'[6] or 'multicultural writer'[7]), so too does Janaczewska refuse to be contained by the safe, if arbitrary, limits of genre. In 2010, in response to a perceived 'crisis' in Australian playwriting, Janaczewska mused:

Playwriting is going through a transition as performance writers work with, and respond to, our ever-shifting digital environment, to post-dramatic theatre and to a whole host of other cultural forces. Along with colleagues, I'm finding that I'm writing fewer narrative dramas and developing instead modular scripts, open texts, plays with unattributed dialogue and minimal or no stage directions and more works [that] combine essayistic and documentary elements, drawn from other [non-theatrical] performance forms. On the page these plays look quite different from their more traditional counterparts and are therefore, perhaps, easy to dismiss [as] not proper plays.[8]

As she notes here, the risk is that the gatekeepers of theatre culture will not recognise the potential of new forms and approaches which extend and reinvigorate theatre as an artform. And yet, this is hardly a new departure for Janaczewska. In 1998 she contributed to a collection of contemporary fictocritical prose. Amanda Nettelbeck, editor of that volume, suggests that fictocriticism might 'most usefully be defined as hybridized writing that moves between the poles of fiction ("invention"/"speculation") and criticism ("deduction"/"explication"), of subjectivity ("interiority") and objectivity ("exteriority"). It is writing that brings the "creative" and the "critical" together [...] mutating both'.[9] It is, Nettelbeck claims, 'not just a "genre"; more than that, it is a way of speaking, a mode of performance".[10]

Indeed—characterised by the fragmentary, self-reflexivity, inter-textuality, the bending of narrative boundaries, crossing of genres and adaptation of literary forms—these elements of fictocriticism, identified by Nettelbeck, are also characteristic of much of Janaczewska's writing for performance. In this volume, *Good with Maps* takes the essay form as its initiating premise, but melds it into a new performative mode; *Teacup in a Storm* both draws on and extends the genre of verbatim theatre.

Be adventurous ... *Good with Maps*

This play takes adventure as its starting point—both in structure and theme. Originally performed by Janaczewska herself (with direction and dramaturgy by Kathryn Millard) in 2011, *Good with Maps* was shortlisted for the Rodney Seaborn Playwrights Award in that year. Its first full production (performed by Jane Phegan) was at Kings Cross Theatre in 2016, directed by Kate Gaul for Siren Theatre Company. The production was warmly received ('*Good with Maps* is one of those rare and beautiful productions I dream about, where a fine writer has handed a text to a fine director who calls forth a great performance from a fine actor who inspires creatives around her to produce their best for the show'[11]) and Gaul was nominated for Best Direction in the 2016 Sydney Theatre Awards for her production, alongside Nate Edmondson who won the award for Best Score or Sound Design. (Janaczewska had stipulated that 'a soundscape is an integral and important component of the piece': her work is frequently and richly informed by a deep knowledge and appreciation of the often overlooked aural possibilities of both sound and music in performance.[12]) *Good with Maps* was then produced at the Edinburgh Fringe Festival in 2017, again to critical acclaim.

Janaczewska describes this work as 'my monologue cum performance essay',[13] 'performance essay' being a term she has coined 'to describe a hybrid which draws not only on the essay and the monologue, but also on field reports, memoir, spoken word, cultural criticism, reportage and the tradition of the illustrated lecture'.[14] It is, she claims, 'a protean and accommodating genre' and Janczewska is clearly resisting *Good with Maps*' containment solely within the box of 'dramatic monologue'. This is with good reason, if we consider the expansive possibilities of the essay form, especially when harnessed to performance. Jeff Porter, for example, has asserted that 'the trademark of the essay is its intimacy, the human voice addressing an imagined audience'.[15]

In Janaczewska's work, of course, the audience is both imagined (in the process of writing) and present (in the performance—and especially where the writer performs her own work), and the intimacy generated is the very particular, communal one between writer/performer and audience members. Robert Manne has also suggested that 'an essay is a reasonably short piece of prose in which we hear a distinctive voice attempting to recollect or illuminate or explain one or another aspect of the world … with an essay, we trust that the distinctive voice we hear is truthful or authentic, even when perhaps it is not'.[16] So ubiquitous is this convention that one reviewer of *Good with Maps* confessed to being disconcerted—'put out'—by discovering after the performance that the writer had not been the performer.[17] Maria Tumarkin—with whom I suspect Janaczewska might well be in sympathy—has written that essays:

> are for picking up ideas, forces in the air, still unnamed and amorphous, and giving them a foothold in language. Whatever is in the air and whatever is disappearing—unnoticed, unmourned. They are for resisting choices offered to us that are not true, yet made to seem inescapable ... And they are for picking sides of barricades when it is morally imperative to do so. In an essay, you can take something that happened to you, or to the girl/cat/tree over there, and make a larger space for this experience, so that it may connect up with the experiences of others, but also with the flows of history, politics, culture, science.[18]

This maps clearly on to what Janaczewska is attempting here. 'Essay', of course, comes from the French noun 'essai' and verb 'essayer'—to attempt, to try (out), to experiment: a form well suited, then, to her adventurous excursion. (Not her first, incidentally, as intrepid explorer: in an earlier work—a proto-performance essay and perhaps prequel to *Good with Maps*—Janaczewska performed her monologue *F.R.G.S.* [Fellow of the Royal Geographic Society] at Griffin Theatre Company in Sydney in 2007. That production included PowerPoint projections 'referencing the tradition of the blog, the "slide night" and those illustrated lectures given by many explorers on their return'.[19])

Good with Maps documents the narrator—'Noëlle (or other performer)'—who is 'good with maps', on her journey up the Amazon River, and simultaneously her father's last journey, suffering with Parkinson's, towards death. Travelogue, history lesson filled with adventurers past, memoir and more, underpinning this monologue is a lifelong passion for literature, its joys and its solaces. *Good with Maps* opens and closes with an evocation of Joseph Conrad, that well-travelled Polish-British seaman and novelist who even reached Australia in the late nineteenth century, perhaps in a nod to Janaczewska's own trajectory through life.

Her own literary skills are particularly evident in this performance essay: it is exceptionally carefully crafted, and the apparent stream-of-consciousness flow belies a rigorous seeding of ideas, the placement and juxtaposition of aural, visual and literary cues for the audience, and a delicate weaving together of the threads of her narrative/s. Floating in the Amazon, for example, admiring the clouds, our narrator notes that 'Out of the blue, formations shaped like giant cauliflowers boil up and turn in on themselves'. The next paragraph begins 'When I lived in the Blue Mountains...' and concludes with a rumination on the 'turquoise line', the Amazon, 'wiggling its way from the Andes to the Atlantic' in her school atlas: in one short passage we've ranged over centuries, continents, geography and history, all with the colour blue sounding our progress throughout. Several pages later Janaczewska tells us the story of a nineteenth-century adventurer who died 'an octogenarian in England' and this slips to her next thought: 'My mother phoned: my father was very ill'. The two moments frame and inform one another—the one pre-empting her own elderly father's death in England; the other implicitly connecting him back to an intrepid expeditioner. Janaczewksa makes many of these connections for us—and, I would suggest, her rich texts invite us to make our own. For me, for example, her evocation of her father as 'an immigrant on the threshold of a vast night' almost inevitably conjured Dylan Thomas's famous poem 'Do not go gentle into that good night'—and from there my own free-associating took me to another Currency Press author and outstanding Australian playwright, Patricia Cornelius, and her play, *Do Not Go Gentle*.[20] That play is set in a nursing home where its residents, at the end of their own life journeys, play out a parallel story of bravery and adventure, Scott's doomed expedition to the South Pole: the connection back to *Good with Maps* is satisfying.

Performance essays by other artists are often closely aligned with the autobiographical or the documentary, and a sense of 'authenticity' in its intentions and execution is clearly perceived by critics as somehow further validating such material. Another reviewer, for example, warmly endorsed the production of *Good with Maps* as '[a] fine performance, delivered from the heart in a way that seems authentically autobiographical'.[21] Janaczewska melds/melts both autobiography and documentary, along with the literary, into her own self-claimed and mapped territory here (and with scant interest in the 'authentic' as a compelling consideration in her composition). In *Teacup in a Storm*, the literary and the documentary are also in play, and expectations unsettled or inverted (as from the outset, in its title), though with a different emphasis.

Dare to be unfashionable ... *Teacup in a Storm*

Janaczewska has stated that much of her work 'deals with history's gaps and silences, focusing on people, plants, creatures and events overlooked or marginalised in official records'.[22] In this play, the often hidden, and certainly unfashionable, world of carers—'people who care for a partner, parent, friend or family member with a disability or enduring health need'[23]—is revealed to us through ten characters and 'multiple other voices'. The *Teacup in a Storm* project was initiated by Therese Cook, a performer and carer, who interviewed fellow carers in the Blue Mountains/Penrith area of Sydney. These stories then formed the basis of a two-week collaborative creative development workshop with performer/devisors Therese Cook and Marie Chanel, director/devisor Nick Atkins and Janaczewska as writer/devisor. Following the workshop Janaczewska wrote a 'modular' script, and during rehearsal for the first production (by The Q/Joan Sutherland Performing Arts Centre in 2016) that script was then 'cut and pasted and compiled into the play', and performed by Cook and Chanel.[24] Janaczewska won an AWGIE Award in 2017 for Community and Youth Theatre for *Teacup in a Storm*.

Verbatim theatre—where a play is constructed from the precise words of people on the public record, and/or who have been interviewed about a particular topic or event—has become an increasingly popular theatrical genre in recent years. Janaczewska's play goes beyond the strict parameters of verbatim practice to create a mix of documentary material and fictional framing narrative, drawing on the tropes of fairytales and nursery rhymes. While some would argue that the strength of verbatim is in its claim to unadulterated 'truth', *Teacup in a Storm* moves us into another realm where the unsung, unpaid, invisible and critically important work of carers[25] is dignified, not only by its public presentation, but also by this play's implicit declaration of its worthiness for staging in, in the words of director/devisor Nick Atkins, 'a heightened poetic style of performance'.[26] Atkins has noted that this indeed was critical for its first audiences:

> We considered if a carer was to receive only three hours of respite a fortnight and they chose to attend our performance, what could we offer them? A documentary piece seemed to fall short of all we wanted to share.[27]

INTRODUCTION

One reviewer gave due credit to the creators who had 'listened with great compassion and empathy and who wrote and performed with such sensitivity and understanding',[28] and thereby identified a crucial element of this play. Just as the sound design was an 'integral and important'[29] component of *Good with Maps*, so too does *Teacup in a Storm* rely on intense listening as a thematic, structuring and indeed instructional (in a non-didactic way!) element of the play. As well as the voices of the 'real' people set down in the script, we also catch wisps of fairytales—those archetypal stories that were our first listenings as children when we existed in pure sound before we could read ourselves; stories that coached us in the need to do and be good ... and warned us that calamity might still befall us. Sound is also used in an almost filmic way in this play, where the crash of one carer's wineglass is simultaneously a jump cut to the 'crash' of a cared-for person floundering in a bathroom. And this play openly invites us to listen hard: to listen to those stories we have ignored because they are inconvenient, painful and have no guaranteed 'happy ever after'—and also because sometimes there is. As 'Patrick' states: 'People say that he's a very lucky boy to have found me. I say I think I'm a very lucky man that I found him'.

One of the most striking elements of *Teacup in a Storm* is indeed Janaczewksa's skilful juxtaposition of the routines and domesticity of daily life—cups of tea and loads of laundry are repeated images in the play—with the mytho-poetic world of fairytales. Her play brings home to us in startling and powerful ways that these core stories of our culture, stories we embrace rather than shy away from, are also replete with children at risk, inadequate parents, difficult elders, the non-neurotypical (the Princess and the Pea), the differently abled (Thumbelina), the long-term physically incapacitated (Sleeping Beauty).

Good with Maps and *Teacup in a Storm* are companion pieces in so far as they both deal with the consequences of debility—but this would be the thinnest and most prosaic possible interpretation of these plays and their significance. Let us say, rather, that they are about human journeys—even 'Lindsey' in *Teacup in a* Storm says, 'When I'm feeling good I see it as a journey'. Grand and small, historical and contemporary, domestic and mythical, paths we might tread in daily life or in our mind's eye. And it is through the work of artists that we can see, and better understand, ourselves on those journeys. The last word here, then, should go to the author herself:

I'm fascinated by language, its power to shape, limit and transform our personal and public lives ... As a dramatist, I'm drawn to society's fault-lines, its points of tension and contradiction. The spaces, both literal and imaginary, where different traditions and worldviews come into contact; those areas of community and individual life that are in flux or transition, because I think these are the areas and interactions that reveal the most about a society.[30]

Laura Ginters

Laura Ginters is Senior Lecturer in the Department of Theatre and Performance Studies at the University of Sydney. She also works as a script assessor and dramaturg, and her play translations have been produced, published and adapted, including for Belvoir St Theatre, Malthouse Theatre and the Sydney Theatre Company.

---

[1] Noëlle Janaczewska. *Storyline*, No. 34, Mar 2014: 94-97 https://search.informit.com.au/documentSummary;dn=225090423214787;res=IELAPA

[2] Joanne Tompkins. 2013. 'Noëlle Janaczewska's Twenty-First Century Theatre: Explorations of Australian Cultural Constructs and Theatrical Form', pp207-220 in Richard Fotheringham and James Smith, eds. *Catching Australian Theatre in the 2000s*. Amsterdam & New York: Rodopi, p208.

[3] Her awards include the Queensland Premier's Literary Award (*Mrs Petrov's Shoe*), the Playbox-Asialink Playwriting Competition, the Griffin Award (*Songket*) and no fewer than seven AWGIE (Australian Writers' Guild) awards for her works for radio, as well as one for theatre: at the time of publication her most recent radio work, *Seoul City Sue* has been nominated for an AWGIE. In 2014 Janaczewska was also the recipient of Yale University's prestigious Windham Campbell Prize which recognised her body of dramatic writing.

[4] Matthew Westwood. 2014. 'Playwright delights in windfall prize surprise'. *The Australian*. 10 March.

[5] Noëlle Janaczewska. 2018. 'Production Notes' in *Good with Maps and Teacup in a Storm*, Sydney: Currency Press, p4.

[6] Noëlle Janaczewska. 1987. '"Do We Want a Piece of the Cake? Or Do We Want to Bake a Whole New One?" Feminist Theatre in Britain'. *Hecate* 13:1 (May 31) 106-112 at 106.

[7] She has noted that she would be 'very unhappy' to be labelled '"a feminist

writer" or a "multicultural writer" or indeed any other label besides "writer"'. See Kerrie Schaefer and Laura Ginters. 2001. "'The more things change the more they stay the same…"? Feminisms and Performance Studies'. *Australasian Drama Studies* (October) 39 104-124 at 114.

[8] In Alison Croggon. 2010. 'Performance Anxiety: Is Australian Playwriting in Crisis?' *The Australian Literary Review*, 2 June.

[9] Amanda Nettelbeck. 1998. 'Notes Towards an Introduction', pp1-17 in Heather Kerr and Amanda Nettelbeck, eds. *The Space Between: Australian Women Writing Fictocriticism*. Nedlands (WA): University of Western Australia Press, pp3-4. Janaczewska's contribution muses on lemons, love, life and literature—to name but a few topics ('Lemon Pieces' ['Quelques Morceaux en Forme de Citron'], pp53-68).

[10] Amanda Nettelbeck. 1998. 'Notes Towards an Introduction', pp1-17 in Heather Kerr and Amanda Nettelbeck, eds. *The Space Between: Australian Women Writing Fictocriticism*. Nedlands (WA): University of Western Australia Press, p6.

[11] Lisa Thatcher, '*Good with Maps*. Journeys Without Within and Through Time'. https://lisathatcher.com/2016/11/14/good-with-maps-journeys-without-within-and-through-time-theatre-review/

[12] See also Laura Ginters. 2005. 'Radio Drama as Music Theatre? Re-defining a Genre in Plays by Noëlle Janaczewska', in: *Radio in the World* (Proceedings of The Radio Conference 2005). Melbourne: RMIT Publishing: 482-92: http://search.informit.com.au/documentSummary;dn=039687635993131;res=E-LIBRARY

[13] https://noelle-janaczewska.com/2016/10/05/good-with-maps-sydney-season/

[14] https://noelle-janaczewska.com/about

[15] Jeff Porter. 2012. 'Introduction: A History and Poetics of the Essay', pp ix-xxiv in Jeff Porter and Patricia Foster, eds. *Understanding the Essay*. Ontario: Broadview Press, p.ix.

[16] Robert Manne. 2014. 'Introduction', pp13-18 in Robert Manne, ed. *The Best Australian Essays 2014*. Melbourne: Black Inc, p14.

[17] See: David James, 'Good with Maps' http://www.londoncitynights.com/2017/08/edinburgh-fringe-good-with-maps-at-c.html%20 (6 August 2017): 'I only realised after the show that the writer (Noëlle Janaczewska) wasn't actually performing the piece. Rather, it was performed by an actor. I accept that this is a bizarre criticism, but I was a little put out at this. I was properly emotionally invested in what Jane Phegan was saying and easily assumed she was talking about her own life, leaving me feeling a bit short-changed when I realised that every little hitch in her voice and moment of weakness was a performance.'

[18] Maria Tumarkin. 2015. 'What the essayist spills', *Sydney Review of Books*, 2

December. https://sydneyreviewofbooks.com/the-unspeakable-meghan-daum/
[19] Noëlle Janaczewska. 2009. F.R.G.S., pp25-31 in *Short Circuit. 14 Short Plays for the Stage*. Sydney: Currency Press, p26.
[20] Patricia Cornelius. 2011. *Do Not Go Gentle* and *The Berry Man*. Sydney: Currency Press.
[21] http://www.edinburghguide.com/festival/2017/theatre/drama/goodwithmapscprimoreview-18181
[22] https://noelle-janaczewska.com/about/
[23] Noëlle Janaczewska. 2018. 'Synopsis', *Teacup in a Storm*. Original manuscript.
[24] https://noelle-janaczewska.com/2016/02/12/teacup-in-a-storm/ Many of Janaczewska's works (such as *The Marie Curle Chat Show* or *Slowianska Street* to give just two examples) are written flexibly and may be performed by large companies of actors: *Teacup in a Storm* similarly, while first performed by only two actors, 'lends itself to larger cast production and features a majority of female roles'. Janaczewska further invites theatre-makers to 'feel free to cast in favour of cultural diversity'. (Noëlle Janaczewska. 2018. 'Characters/Voices' in *Good with Maps and Teacup in a Storm*. Sydney: Currency Press, p34)
[25] One in eight Australians is a carer; carers perform 1.9 billion hours of unpaid work every year. See: 'The Economic Value of Informal Care in Australia in 2015'. Deloitte Access Economics Report: http://www.carersaustralia.com.au/storage/Access%20Economics%20Report.pdf. See also: Andrew Taylor, 'Teacup in a Storm: Caring for the unsung, unpaid heroes whose stories we ignore', *Sydney Morning Herald*, 22 February 2016.
[26] Andrew Taylor, 'Teacup in a Storm: Caring for the unsung, unpaid heroes whose stories we ignore', *Sydney Morning Herald*, 22 February 2016.
[27] Nick Atkins, 'Media Release: *Teacup in a Storm*'. http://jacquibonnermarketing.com/wp-content/uploads/2016/01/MEDIA-RELEASE-Teacup-in-a-Storm-2016-at-The-Joan_Approved.pdf
[28] Carol Wimmer, *Teacup in a Storm* http://www.stagewhispers.com.au/reviews/teacup-storm
[29] Noëlle Janaczewksa. 2018. 'Production Notes' in G*ood with Maps and Teacup in a Storm*. Sydney: Currency Press, p4.
[30] http://www.currency.com.au/No%C3%ABlle-Janaczewska-playwright-interview.aspx

Good with Maps

For my father, 1923–2008

Good With Maps was first produced by Siren Theatre Company at the Kings Cross Theatre, Sydney, on 8 November 2016, with the following cast:

    Performer   Jane Phegan

Director and Producer, Kate Gaul
Designer, Alice Morgan
Composer and Sound Designer, Nate Edmondson
Lighting Designer, Louise Mason
Stage Manager, Zara Thompson

Good With Maps was researched and written with a New Work grant from the Literature Board of the Australia Council.

PRODUCTION NOTES

Good With Maps is a monologue-cum-performance essay. A soundscape is an integral and important component of the piece. Other than that, its staging requirements are basic—but absolutely no sofas.

Layout and punctuation suggest rhythm and delivery. The piece can be read instead of memorised, or done with some combination of both.

Some or all of the books quoted on pages 9, 10, 19, 23 and 31 may or may not be incorporated into the production.

There are two things to know about me: I'm a freshwater person not a beach person, and I'm good with maps. Bloody good, in fact. Give me a map and I'll get there.

Without a map, my father told me during one of those long drives of childhood, there's no way of knowing where we are. There is no here without there, he said, no world without a map. Sometimes they guide you, sometimes they transport you.

He passed me the road atlas. And with it, the responsibility.

Right now it's 8:35 a.m. and I'm waiting on the jetty for a boat that's going to take me upriver to the world's largest fluvial archipelago. On the Rio Negro almost a hundred kilometres from its confluence with the Rio Solimões and the Amazon mainstream.

Here it comes, a tramp steamer, like something out of a story by Joseph Conrad—except it's not. It's a motor launch equipped with life jackets, mini-fridge and a tour guide.

Beat.

An Australian waterway is a tenuous thing, and in England where I grew up, the countryside is crosshatched with streams you can jump across. Nothing remotely like the Amazon. Which was an abstraction, something viewed from the living room across a distance of carpet and television.

Until now.

It's January, we're about a dozen people on the boat, and I'm struggling with the language.

I'm catching approximately half the commentary. Like this:

One. The Amazon is halfway between high-water maximum and its dry-season low.

Two. Something or other in rapid-fire Portuguese.

Three. Piranhas are misunderstood. They're not ferocious, blood-hungry carnivores. Current studies suggest they have a nervous disposition and huddle in frightened shoals to avoid predators who would eat *them* alive—

A few hours later we're cooling off with a swim in the river, so I hope we can trust those scientists.

I'm floating on my back looking up at the sky.

More than the river, more than wildlife, it's the dramatic cloudscapes of the Amazon that grab my attention. Out of the blue, formations shaped like giant cauliflowers boil up and turn in on themselves. Change colour, and draw their shadows across the water.

When I lived in the Blue Mountains one my favourite walks took me to a point where there was no obvious sign of human presence. If I block out my fellow passengers and their cameras, I can do the same here:

Pretend I'm seeing the Amazon as the first Europeans did.

Beginning with Francisco de Orellana in 1542, a steady stream of explorers sailed in search of El Dorado, miracle beasts, personal glory, or—in the case of Isabela Godin in 1769—a husband. But in our classroom the Amazon remained relatively unexplored.

We recited the measurements: over a thousand tributaries, twenty per cent of the freshwater discharge into the world's oceans, et cetera. But the narratives of adventure and conquest we learnt were British. South America was Latin America and therefore off the map so to speak.

Yet my *Philips' Concise Atlas* always fell open at page one-two-two. My gaze always alighted on that turquoise line wiggling its way from the Andes to the Atlantic.

And now, decades later, I've finally landed on that page.

Three degrees south of the equator, Manaus is an oddity: a city of two million in the heart of the Amazon. On paper it's six bold-face letters amid a swathe of green; on the ground, the humidity is crushing.

'Because of the evaporation, Manaus is always evaporating,' the taxi driver explained as he ferried me from the airport.

Travel websites describe Manaus as dirty and traffic-clogged, an oily blot on our rainforest fairytales. They advise moving on to greener pastures a.s.a.p. But I like the buzz and frontier ambience of this river port.

The slipways and weathered cargo vessels hark back to what I think of as a favourite British pastime: reading about dogged, upright gentlemen suffering in appalling conditions while searching for a pole, an inland sea, or a fellow explorer gone AWOL. Ripping yarns and travelogues where blokes wrangle crocodiles, hostile natives, tumultuous oceans—and their own natures.

Here's an example from 1931:

'... *tall trees stretched soft fingers towards the skies ... By my side were men whose histories I knew, men who had been dissatisfied with the comforts of civilization and who had taken to the wilds in the hope of fortune certainly, but more I suspect from the terrible regularity of meals.*' *

What's contemporary adventure porn? Billionaires in balloons? Teenagers in yachts? Reality TV playing Robinson Crusoe? Or maybe those memoirs where women go to Italy or Asia looking for a decent meal and a bit of spiritual whatnot. Instead of charting mountain ranges, our heroine charts her emotions; instead of surviving a locust plague, she survives

heartbreak

or the indifference of the villagers.

Not my kind of quest.

Not my cup of chai.

Although ...

I'm no fan of those early twentieth-century action men, but I have to

---

* *Green Hell*, Julian Duguid: The Century Co., c1931.

confess a sneaking admiration for that very British breed of nut case who treats flood, pestilence or meltdown as a minor inconvenience and refuses to bend.

There's no need to evacuate, consult a doctor, or make a fuss.

Works the same for windfalls. Lottery winners who decide to keep their day job in the factory.

> *Beat.*

Saw the map, bought the book.

I'm a sucker

for those books that come with a map tucked between the title page and preface. Sketch maps at the front of kids' classics, the layouts of crime fiction, or the city plans that introduce us to Andrei Bely's *Petersburg*.

This fantastic novel of linguistic invention and murky yellow mists was recommended to me by a friend: 'If you like Gogol,' she said, 'you must read Bely.' So I did.

And the surprise is, although it was published in 1913, this not-terribly-well-known work of Russian modernism is strikingly postmodern in its treatment of space.

'There is no Petersburg. It only appears to exist.' *

Back to the Amazon, which is big—literally and metaphorically.

Always has been.

It ignited the passions of biologists and conquistadores, inspired hundreds of utopian dreamings and get-rich-quick schemes, became the poster standard of the environmental movement. And it loomed large in my first career plan:

to be an explorer.

At Goff's Oak County Primary, and later at high school, I'd wander off into elaborate daydreams about the adventures that would be mine when I left the pebble dash and boredom of Goff's Oak.

---

* *Petersburg*, Andrei Bely, trans. John Elsworth: Pushkin Press, 2009.

A lifetime's drift began. The urge to get up and go, escape the reach of home, the desire to be

elsewhere.

At university I joined the Exploration Club hoping to further this ambition. But the only place I went was to their annual dinner where I sat next to a chap called something like Rupert Hattersly-Adams. 'Call me Hatters,' he said. He had a red face like a monkey's arse and he told me about his last odyssey. 'Kohistan—can you imagine?' And I could. I could imagine him trekking the North-West Frontier complete with pith helmet and Royal Doulton tea service.

I've moved on since then, but the Amazon stayed

fixed in my mind as the ultimate destination,

and now here I am:

Slapping at insects as our guide explains riparian symbiosis in Portuguese too complicated for me to follow.

I zone out,

follow a dragonfly instead,

watch it alight on a hunk of polystyrene bobbing in a rip.

We're moving again, downriver, and as the banks diverge, everything broadens and falls away leaving this enormous space overhead. Cloud masses move like a time lapse, with energetic shifts of light and texture. I take photos of them and that evening, email a selection to my father.

 Beat.

I should have seen it coming,

but I didn't.

And I blame email. That's another thing you should know about me: I don't like phone chat. If face-to-face isn't possible, I prefer the written word. Especially when it comes to my parents. They're from that generation when phone calls between England and Australia cost an arm and a leg, and although times have changed, and I've explained that times have changed, they haven't. So we'd have these stilted dialogues, and often the technology would add to the awkwardness with echoes and delays in which I'd hear my own voice bounce back at me.

Until Dad discovered the Internet.

My mother refused to go anywhere near a computer, but Dad embraced the online world with gusto

and I replied,

'... Hope you're well, lots of love, Noëlle [*or other performer's name*].'

'Mustn't grumble,' he'd type. 'Only the aches and pains one might expect at my age.'

And so on and so I didn't realise that all was not well until I received a birthday card. Special occasions and the trimmings were my mother's remit, but this time it was Dad who'd sent the card.

His handwriting had become small and squirrely.

I hit the phone.

'Dad? It's me, Noëlle [*or other performer's name*]. How are you?'

The silence that followed was the sound of thoughts at sea, thrown off course, sucked into gaps, flailing as they tumbled.

Finally there was engagement, like a piece of film catching, holes locking onto ratchets

—

Dad started talking about Tesco.

I need to detour here.

Like many people, I grew up in a crap place. My particular crap place was south-east Hertfordshire, seventeen miles north of London. Think ring-roads and shopping centres stretching all the way to the horizon. Where you can't see the woods for the acres of car parks. Sure, the county has hamlets with names like Barleycroft End and

Hogpits Bottom, but they lay north and west on the white spaces of the map, as remote as the Amazon—or Australia, for that matter. The bit of Hertfordshire I grew up in was Goff's Oak, a suburban village midway between stockbroker belt and Cheshunt.

Semi-detached, semi-conscious, semi-the-same, chocolate-sprinkles, milk-semi-skimmed-and-always-tepid Cheshunt.

Streets that sprawl along the Lea Valley. A river punctuated by sewage farms and filled-in gravel pits.

Before Victoria Beckham—another Goff's Oak girl—gravel was the area's best-known export.

Ironically however, for a place crammed with roads, there was no public transport to speak of, perhaps because there was nowhere to go, and nothing to do when you got there. So as teenagers we hung about, waiting to be overtaken by—by something. Please God, something!

Tesco is a UK supermarket chain which branched out from groceries to sell the kitchen sink, financial services, and pretty much everything else. The company headquarters were in nearby Cheshunt, and one summer holiday I spent a few weeks there cooking up

scenarios of romance and escape when I should have been filing invoices.

Despite my underperformance however, Tesco continued to ring up huge profits—

and for years Dad's kept his own mental file of complaints:

from corporate greed to misplaced apostrophes ...

But I'm not hearing any of that; I'm hearing an erratic vibrato; I'm hearing his voice getting lost.

I can peruse a map for hours. It's satisfying to pinpoint Surinam and learn that Nauru was once Pleasant Island. And if I ever meet someone from the Azores, I'll know exactly where to place them.

Maps represent our need to know

what lies beyond.

They tell us how to get there, and how to find our way back if beyond turns out to be not terribly nice.

My father liked maps. He'd started out with technical drawing and an interest in cartography, but ended up in education. Although he acquired his post-grad qualifications when the humanities began to collapse into one another, he escaped the maelstrom—because he had a map. He was committed to the idea of real places.

And for all its ability to photosynthesise the fantasies and fears of outsiders, the Amazon is a real place.

During the nineteenth century for example, with its monopoly on latex, one of the industrial revolution's essential ingredients, the region was no more untethered from time than Newcastle or Detroit.

Latex is the milky sap of a tree known by botanists as *Hevea brasiliensis*, and by the layperson as the rubber or weeping tree. It was the basis of the rubber boom, a Brazilian Belle Époque centred on Manaus. Forty-odd years of excess when entrepreneurs and bosses lived in outlandish luxury.

When horses were given champagne to quench their thirst,

ladies mixed cocktails with diamonds instead of ice,

and dirty laundry was sent to Paris or London to be washed.

Although I wonder about these stories which seem to become more baroque with each retelling.

And I wonder about the other side of the coin. Indigenous communities pressed into slavery. The migrants and bonded labourers who poured in and were left stranded when boom went bust.

How it all went wrong is a tale of skulduggery and subterfuge—according to Leandro, our tour guide. 'Henry Wickham destroyed the Amazon,' he says, staring straight at me, the only non-Brazilian on the boat.

He's referring to the Englishman who smuggled seventy thousand seeds of the rubber tree to the Royal Botanic Gardens at Kew in 1876.

Although fewer than four thousand germinated, they were enough to kickstart plantations in the colonies and thereby transfer control of rubber production to Britain.

Wickham himself was one of those Victorian characters who crop up again and again on the edges of the world's maps. A jack-of-all-trades with a talent for self-promotion.

After delivering his purloined seeds, he and his wife set sail for a new life in Queensland, where for ten years or thereabouts, he tried his luck growing tobacco and coffee.

'We danced on his grave when he died!' pronounced Leandro.

I don't point out the logical impossibility of this. That Henry Wickham dodged the vengeance of Brazil to die an octogenarian in England.

But I do feel guilty—

My mother phoned: my father was very ill.

I rescheduled work and flew to England a couple of days later, hoping for the best and fearing the worst.

It was both.

Better because Dad wasn't about to die—and worse because there was something seriously wrong with his motor functioning. His stride had become a shuffle, his hands were frustrated by pens and cutlery, it took a geological age for him to dress himself.

My mother put on a brave face.

Their GP said it was just old age.

I went into overdrive: I organised a gardener, a weekly cleaning service, quotes to install a stair lift. I threw out cracked china and replaced it with new stuff. I contacted social services. I hassled doctors and demanded second—and third—opinions.

My mother accused me of making a scene, and that most heinous of crimes: being rude to a doctor.

—

I grabbed the car keys and stormed out.

I drove down lanes musty with pollen. I drove past intersections where as teenagers we hitched lifts with random blokes. I circled roundabouts looking for a way out only to find myself in Tesco.

Where I stood in the stationery aisle. Unable to see to the other side. Frightened by my incompetence and furious with my parents for putting me in this situation. For hauling me to the other side of the world—and then refusing to do what I told them.

I picked up a multipack of erasers …

If only I could outsource them to India—

Call centres, IT, elective surgery, why not aged care?

I defended myself to an imaginary audience:

'Look, I've tried my best, I really have. They appreciate the elderly in India. They have sunshine, their food is so much better. And, and, and—'

Crash!

> *Beat.*

A feral toddler pulled over a display. Folders, crayons, wishful thinking sent flying.

It was oddly comforting, that mess on the floor. Life isn't all grand passions and noble quests. Some of the time, our feelings are petty rather than profound. Our spirits mean instead of generous, our aspirations mundane, our questions banal. Sometimes, our inner self—or perhaps it's just mine?—is sullen, irritable, childish. You sigh, you check the fridge, you play with your iPhone when your mother is talking to you.

Most Russian novels I've read are soaked in pessimism, and until I came across Gogol, I assumed that was the norm. Russian authors were men—or occasionally women—of tremendous sorrows.

But Gogol is a comic writer, and *Dead Souls* is a great work about how shallow humankind can be.

And there I was,

frozen in the supermarket, ruminating on Russian literature and how art isn't all moral dilemmas and urgent themes.

'Excuse me, madam.'

A Tesco staffer arrived to restore order.

Put everything back to normal.

Why this need to seem normal no matter what? What's wrong with being agitated? With emotions spilling over?

Beat.

I'm going the wrong way.

Upstream when I want to go downriver to Santarém, and from there south on the Rio Tapajós to the curiosity that is Fordlândia.

Amazonia has always attracted people with madcap projects, from the fictional Fitzcarraldo to the very real Daniel Ludwig, who in 1978 had an entire Japanese pulp mill towed across the Pacific and up the Amazon. You can see it arrive on YouTube.

His mission was the development of a massive timber empire growing 'super-trees' from Burma. When they proved unviable he switched to pine and eucalyptus. That didn't work out either, and his billion-dollar dream became a nightmare.

Fordlândia is the spectacular failure of another American capitalist.

In 1927 automobile tycoon Henry Ford decided to smash the British cartel and produce his own rubber. From his office in Michigan, he set about imposing his will on a vast tract of the Amazon. His vision encompassed not only plantations, but the establishment of a town called Fordlândia. A slice of apple-pie America in the midst of the rainforest. Complete with golf course, Tidy Garden contests, and a dance hall in which only music approved by Henry himself was permitted. Any tune you like as long as it's a waltz.

Or maybe a square dance.

Tangos, foxtrots, the charleston and other jazz-age hits were off the playlist. He believed their sensuous rhythms and sliding notes revealed Jewish origins.

Anti-Semitic, anti-union, anti-history, anti-intellectual—there's a lot to dislike about Henry Ford. Not least his disdain for reading. 'Book-sickness,' he said, 'is a modern ailment.'

Dear Dad ... I email my father from Manaus. I mention that I'm hoping to visit the ruins of Fordlândia. We both like follies, and Fordlândia is folly on a truly magnificent scale. His illness makes typing a slow process, so his reply is brief: Go!

I went

to find out:

How long will it take to get to Santarém? No, I don't want to fly. Yes, I know mosquitoes are an issue. No, I'm not looking for a tour package. Just a straightforward boat. Thanks for the brochures, but I—Really, no. I'm sure the six-day safari's wonderful, but it's not—Yes, I like animals, but—birds as well, but what I'm after is the regular trip— Okay, maybe later the eco lodge—No, definitely not a sportfishing cruise—Yes, Barcelos looks magical, but it's three days in the wrong direction. Sorry? I understand there are more mosquitoes that way— But, yes, anyway, I've got your number and—I agree sustainable reservations are good—waterfalls too. Yes, no, maybe if my plans change—thanks again ...

I leave the conditioned atmosphere of the various tourist offices. The central district of Manaus feels compressed.

Gap-year gringos, street hawkers, and

a vast storm system climbing high into the heavens, black with rain.

The dragons and hippogriffs have vanished from the map. Technology has brought home the mystery. Medicine has made harsh environments endurable. By the time I was born, exploration had identified the best routes to connect pretty much all the societies that wanted to be in touch with one another. The blanks have been filled in; there isn't much 'unknown' left. To explore is less an infinitive than a quirky first person, as in: 'I'm going to explore the Great Wall of China backwards in a wheelbarrow.'

As for cartography, forget oxbow lakes and legends. Think a nondescript van trawling suburbia in the name of Google.

Yet exploration goes on.

The downtown internet cafe is busy with anecdotes and competing tales of adversity. Run-ins with drug smugglers and rip-off merchants, lethal frogs, and leeches the size of kittens.

While I wait, it strikes me that in our era of smartphones and social media, travel is becoming less an experience of otherness, and more and more an extension of home life.

'Every year at this season English people made parties which steamed a short way up the river, landed, and looked at the native village, bought a certain number of things from the natives, and returned again without damage done to mind or body.' *

That's Virginia Woolf. You won't find her equatorial America on any map, but her depiction of travellers more involved with each other and the affairs of home than they are with their foreign surroundings is as true today as it was when *The Voyage Out* was published in 1915.

As kids we made-believe there was a geography beyond our own, a *Terra Nostra*, shimmering and sugar-filled.

It began at the corner of Crouch Lane and a weed-choked field called Twenty Acres, which wasn't, and ran north to Rags Brook, which we renamed the Amazon. If we were feeling particularly heroic, we'd ford the Amazon and hack through the jungle to Hammond Street to buy pink candy shrimps with coins we'd 'liberated' from our mothers' purses.

Endangered species, tidal bores, gigantic water lilies ...

---

* *The Voyage Out*, Virginia Woolf: Duckworth, 1915.

It's hard to look at the real thing and not see all the photos and documentaries as well.

And what about the human ecology? The cultural diversity sidelined by this focus on spectacular nature?

The Sephardic Jews and Arab traders, the Japanese agricultural workers and the descendants of African slaves. Indigenous recruits from remote communities off the radar for all but the most intrepid anthropologist now factory-working for Microsoft or Samsung in Manaus.

Another detour:

In the standard history of geography, non-Western explorers are rare creatures. Ditto women.

Jeanne Baret was an accomplished botanist. Disguised as a man she joined Bougainville's expedition in 1766 and became the first woman to circumnavigate the globe.

But at school we did the Captains—Cook and Scott. Then the Sirs—Drake, Franklin, Shackleton. But what I didn't get then and still don't, is why, having gone mad with disease or dehydration, having staggered home barely alive, they immediately plan to go back.

For Mars One volunteers there will be no return. Despite this, the project received over two hundred thousand applicants for its planned one-way mission to the Red Planet.

I was about eight and exploring my father's bookshelves when I came across *Swallows and Amazons*. I settled into an armchair anticipating anacondas and carnivorous flora—only to discover it was set in the English Lake District, not South America. Nevertheless, the tale of kids devising their own adventures without grown-ups getting in the way excited my imagination.

An Outcast of the Islands, Middlemarch, War and Peace ...
In nineteenth-century novels reality was story-shaped.

Until Virginia Woolf came along and blew open the form. Made viewpoints plural and upset that whole beginning-middle-end convention.

While everything in a story moves smoothly, it's not usually like that in real life. Here's what happened.

The emails stopped.

I called my mother. She was coping. Friends and neighbours were marvellous. Yesterday Carol-from-across-the-road brought over a Bakewell tart. My brother and his family were much happier since they'd moved to New Jersey; they'd never really warmed to Michigan. What's the weather like in Sydney? Well, I'll let you get back to your busy life …

And then she rang off. Through the window was a full moon, yellow as an orange. It was cruising up to midnight on this side of the planet. I pictured Dad shuffling from room to room on an obscure mission, an immigrant on the threshold of a vast night. I opened my computer, logged into Qantas-dot-com, and a couple of weeks later arrived in Goff's Oak.

Dad's skin hung in folds, this way and that, his bones jutted, he seemed more chicken soup than grown man.

The situation was teetering toward disaster. My father and mother needed to move or at least accept help, but they, wartime survivors of horrors I can't imagine, were too stoic or too proud to consider it.

I hugged my father and explained that I didn't manage to get to Fordlândia—not this time.

We sipped red wine. His friends and former colleagues dropped by. My mother assured them she was fine, Dad was fine, everything was fine.

More wine?

Dad let slip

his glass.

I mopped up the mess and wondered whether it's parental disintegration that turns us into adults—especially those of us without children.

Towards the end of that visit, Dad took a turn for the worse and was rushed to Chase Farm Hospital.

I was out with a bunch of people I went to school with the night he was admitted, so didn't see him until the following morning.

The hospital had been modernised several times, but there was that whiff of institution and illness that no amount of refurbishment and new technology could quite erase.

It echoed and ticked. Under white fluoros, miscellaneous relatives waited and ate junk food from vending machines. Because it was there.

I took in my father's cubicle, the remains of breakfast, pink sausage, toast barely nibbled, and felt my stomach lurch.

'Has the doctor seen you? What have they said?'

My mother: 'Oh, more tests, you know—'

'No, I don't know. Tests for what? When will we know the results?'

I went to find someone to ask. They were playing Springsteen in the office. None of that edge-of-town, wreck-on-the highway stuff. The 'Dancing in the Dark' years, crunchy guitar riffs and belting sax.

I got some admin person who told me nothing. I already knew enough nothing.

The tests, whatever tests they were, took over a week to come back inconclusive.

A junior medic told me that my father was off the critical list.

I went home.

Now I dreaded the ring of the telephone in the small hours.

In the interim I got tips from friends. I got advice. But above all, we swapped experiences. Some were past tense, some present. Some of us were dealing with nearby crises, some of us were frequent flyers.

A month later Dad was moved to another ward. It sounded grim.

I went back.

It was grim.

So this is old age. A bed, a chair near the television, upholstered in brown to hide the stains. Plastic covers and panic buttons. Handles around the shower, piss-stained underpants in the wash and nurse's aides popping in to see if you're dead yet.

Please flood his nerves with sedatives

and keep him strong enough to crack a smile.

That quote from *King Lear*, Cordelia's line, was playing on a loop inside my head.

'You have begot me, bred me, loved me. I
Return those duties back as are right fit.' *

But was I?

The following day we made arrangements to transfer him out of Chase Farm and into a private hospital.

I went home.

I was still getting over the jet lag when my mother called—finally a diagnosis: Parkinson's.

I hopped online.

Degenerative disorder of central nervous system—mucks up cognitive processes, motor skills—whole heap of mind-boggling medical vocabulary—it's caused by a shortage of neurotransmitter dopamine. No cure, only treatment, and it's going to get a hell of a lot worse before it gets—well, a hell of a lot worse. I scrolled down the list of famous sufferers looking for the most recent research—

Hitler, Franco, Mao Zedong ...

Images of despots gave way to hard-edged discussion of neurological damage and nursing around the clock.

It was two in the morning,

the heart of darkness,

rain was falling in torrents.

---

* *King Lear*, William Shakespeare.

I've always liked rain, the feel of secrecy it engenders, the opportunity it offers to shut out the world.

I made a cup of coffee, delicious organic coffee—probably knitted in one of those jungle outposts.

Outside, clouds heaved, thunder rolled, and a sudden flash of lightning made the furniture in the apartment leap from its shadows.

> *Beat.*

The home which will be my father's home until he comes to his final resting place is in Cheshunt. Purpose-built with generous windows and a sensible garden.

I wonder what it must feel like to go into a place you know you'll never come out of alive.

Of all the explorers who ventured into the Amazon and were never heard from again, the best-known would have to be Colonel Percy Fawcett. Sent initially by the Royal Geographical Society to help Bolivia and Brazil map their border, Fawcett convinced himself that an undiscovered city lay hidden somewhere in the Mato Grosso region. He called his fabled metropolis Z, and in 1925 went off to find it. His disappearance spawned a cottage industry of rumours and rescue campaigns. Film crews and journalists converged on the Amazon to hunt for the Fawcett party. Until the Brazilian government said enough was enough and imposed an embargo.

Fawcett's field notes inspired Arthur Conan Doyle's *The Lost World*. A many-times-adapted-for-film epic where men are men, dinosaurs are dinosaurs, and there was nothing like a rollicking adventure on a distant continent to spark a dull afternoon in Goff's Oak.

In the 1930s Stalin ordered Soviet cartographers to move towns and landmarks. Tourist maps of Moscow and other cities were duly modified.

During the Cold War the KGB compiled maps of enemy territory—including major conurbations in the UK.

These came to light after the collapse of the USSR, when the new Russian government needed fast cash.

Anyway,

the Russians agreed with me:

there was nothing of interest in Goff's Oak.

But they did cover bits of the North London-Hertfordshire overlap, and in extraordinary detail: fire hydrants, the spacing of trees, chalk pits, quarries, pebbles—

Okay, bridges, water depth I get; if you want to sneak a submarine up the River Lea, you need to know it's going to fit. But what's the big deal with rocks?

These Soviet maps were put together from satellite photos, trade directories, the existing Ordnance Survey, and their network of spies on the ground. The idea of a spy ring counting telephone boxes in suburbia makes me laugh. It's so Graham Greene.

I was waiting in the lounge at Sydney's International Terminal. Again. Picking at a plate of cheese and biscuits. Again. Contemplating the wisdom of another glass of wine, listening to the announcement that my flight was delayed. Again.

The article I was reading had a title something like 'Can't See the Wood For the Beasts,' and it was about how millions of hectares of rainforest are being clear-felled to raise beef cattle. I felt helpless, overwhelmed: the Amazon, climate change, rapacious corporations, mortal diseases—

Fortunately, because the last thing I needed was another wallow in feelings of futility, conversation broke out with the announcement of yet a further delay. We started chatting, a group of us waiting for our long-haul flights. Fine at first, but then it was as if we decided the best way to be recognised by one another was via a litany of complaint. Someone griped about the cost of parking; someone else about the catering; the sporting goods salesman bound for Germany droned on about all his other overseas trips and how he'd been robbed at knife-point in Russia, not once, but twice.

I excused myself. What did I have to grizzle about? My father was dying on the other side of the planet ...

I flew back and forth to England to see Dad, and each time I returned there was less of him.

My father looked like his own X-ray.

My mother busied herself with fruit and organising his sweaters. I sat and held his hand.

His life will never be normal again, never be what it was before this malady took hold. Before Parkinson's he was an incurable optimist. He was independent, resourceful, a voracious reader, someone who organised outings, tackled difficult crosswords and visited sick friends. Now he was just another old man who needed visiting and supervision himself.

A collection of toy ships sat on the windowsill like a second childhood.

I tried to conjure more positive images. His trolley bed with its rigging weighs anchor and goes sailing away, past the lighthouse where the night staff hole up with mugs of Nescafé, out into the Straits of Magellan or Malacca.

My mother is a very sociable being, and when she came to see Dad, she'd often nip across the corridor for a chat. Gwen knew more people who'd undergone operations than anyone else and loved to rehearse the particulars of each case with a terrifying command of detail. While Laurie told anyone who'd listen that he almost climbed Mount Everest. Whether this meant he almost reached the summit, or almost joined an expedition, I never discovered, but there was about him an odour of tweed and pipe tobacco.

I suspect the real appeal of Gwen and Laurie was their ability to talk— unlike Dad whose speech was gone. Occasionally he'd utter a few syllables, but they never added up to anything comprehensible.

Did the words get lost in transmission? Somewhere in the contours of his brain? Or if they made it out of the brain did they take a wrong turn before they reached the mouth? If my father could hear the conversation he wanted inside his head, the frustration must be unbearable.

I felt pointless—or do I mean helpless? I too was lost for words, lost for the right words. The ones I wanted were immense and deafening. Problem was: I couldn't locate them, those big words, only platitudes.

That evening, while my mother watched a program about migrating birds, I cooked dinner for us. We ate in front of the TV. Outside I heard someone whistle as they walked their dog. Onscreen, a flock of young swallows followed their magnetic compass to a home they'd never seen.

As a kid, with my school atlas open at the Amazon, I could almost smell the sunlight, heavy and lovely as pineapple.

If the river is about space, the cloudscape is about time. Although Dad was still living at home and semi-competent, when I made my trip to the Amazon, I think on some level I knew that he had begun his own journey to the unknown.

Everybody thought it would last forever.

In 1876, when Wickham made his escape with the seeds of *Hevea brasiliensis*, Dunlop's pneumatic tyre was a decade away, and Henry Ford was thirteen years old.

The collapse took nearly forty years to come.

Rubber plantations took root in South-East Asia, and by the end of the First World War, Manaus was once again a backwater and the dazzle years of the boom a fast-fading memory.

Nowadays the mansions of the erstwhile rubber barons rot in the sodden air,

and if a backpacker buys a condom, it's most likely imported from Malaysia.

Like Leandro, many Brazilians still regard Wickham's seed-snatch as bio-piracy.

Although as a businessman in Manaus explains to me over caipirinhas, Brazil is now earning a tidy profit from hybrid eucalypts. And megabucks from soya beans, a plant which originated in China.

He shrugs off reports of dirty tactics and rampant deforestation as the ravings of eco-fanatics and left-wing troublemakers.

Where some see infinite nature there for the taking, others see a fragile ecosystem. But the Amazon isn't a panacea for global ills. To ring-fence it as primal wilderness and exclude outsiders would be a mistake. Why? Several reasons, but here's one: because it may hold the source material for new drugs that could one day cure diseases—like Parkinson's.

Today the storm broke early.

It lashes buttress roots and dilutes the ground beneath our feet to slop.

My fellow passengers race for shelter, but I'm hot and sweaty and the rain, even warm rain, is refreshing.

After the deluge, the clouds and their passing shadows move on. Torn up by their own violence, they scud off to regroup on some other horizon.

The few days I've got left before I return to Rio, are spent in boats and canoes, exploring—I'd like to say the river less-travelled, but—

'Every visitor discovers the Amazon for themselves,' Leandro tells me. It doesn't matter that someone else got here first. There's enough discovery to go around.

In bookshops and libraries we went our separate ways.

Dad liked military biographies. Serious scholarly ones. Nelson and Napoleon. Wellington, Duke of.

Whereas I've marched miles on anti-war protests—and look—

I can't compete with those armies of white blokes clanking through virgin undergrowth, but I like to think of myself as artistically and intellectually adventurous.

Virginia Woolf felt that reading a novel should be like taking a voyage to a strange land.

In the lobby where I'm staying, an American retiree asks me if I get scared travelling alone.

Right now my biggest fear is being up the Amazon without a book.

I went upstairs to my father's study to riffle his hardbacks. Inside one I found a photo of Dad. In this tiny snap, he's young again and smiling.

Grief has the ability to strip away time. Looking at that image of my father, my adult life dissolved. I was a little girl again, whose small hand fitted easily inside his big one and—

I can feel at home almost anywhere except my native land. And sometimes I wonder if I'm not most at home in a hotel room with a notebook and wi-fi.

You get to an age when all the angst about who you're going to be is over and you're left with—whatever you're left with.

The Amazon on my last night offers no horizon, rolling unbroken into wet, inky infinity. Sky and river in unison. Far out, I can see the silhouettes of tiny boats as they bob among the churning water, like monsters on a medieval map—

I stumble into my father's digital shadow. It's a shock to find him— his research and syntax … all there in the clouds of cyberspace.

In non-virtual reality, he sat hunched up and fragile like eggs. I don't know why I kept comparing him to food, but I did. It was odd, in the way that life is odd but ordinary at the same time.

I sat on a chair like the ones we had in high school.

Dad willed the clock back,

I willed it forward—

or vice versa.

I wished he could say something to me instead of staring. His eyes like haddock beneath the permafrost of levodopa and whatever other prescriptions he was swallowing. But his face didn't move. The synapses of his brain firing in wild uncharted paths where I couldn't follow.

Later: my mother explained. That staring is a symptom of Parkinson's.

Later: when visitors are long gone, the night shift patrols the lanes between dreamers. Those battened down under sheeting. Snorers foghorning through the darkness. And the restless ones, the groaners and channel surfers. Convoys of the unsleeping.

Unlike Dad, my mother has no faith in cartography.

His last visit, my brother put a GPS navigation device in her car. My mother removed it the moment he went back to the States.

I retrieved it from the shed and reinstalled it.

My mother's resilience, the willpower that was holding her together, that was helping her adjust to living alone for the first time in her life, was eroding.

I suggested we take a drive, grab a pub lunch, maybe go for a stroll.

We set off with me in the driving seat

and my mother regaling me with horror stories about GPS systems directing elderly people to drive off cliffs and into canals.

How on earth could a GPS know your age? I opened my mouth to tell her they were urban myths—

and shut it again.

Promised her instead that I wouldn't let technology lead us astray.

The end of my father's life is ugly, messy, undignified. It involves being manipulated onto stretchers and into wheelchairs and decanted into single beds. It involves wearing nappies and spilling cornflakes down the front of your pullover and having to live with it for the rest of the day. It involves people you've never met calling you by your first name as if you're close friends and talking to you as if you are eight rather than eighty-five.

It involves no privacy but too much intimacy of entirely the wrong kind.

Call me insane, but I once dumped a boyfriend over *Moby Dick*. That he hadn't read it was okay, just about. The deal-breaker was that he wasn't interested in reading it. And in the grotty kitchen of that share house in Islington all those years ago, it hit me with harpoon force that I'd inherited more than DNA from my father.

The man who introduced me to Dostoyevsky and Voltaire, the father who invented stories about flies called Aggelrob and Berylton and made bathtub soap scum into a character, the dad who read *The Wind in the Willows* to me, can't read anymore.

So I read to him:

Józef Teodor Konrad Korzeniowski—

that's Joseph Conrad to you.

'The rain began to fall again; first like a wet mist, then with a heavier touch, thickening into a smart, perpendicular downpour; and the hiss and thump of the approaching steamer was coming extremely near ...' *

THE END

---

* *Nostromo: A Tale of the Seaboard*, Joseph Conrad: Harper & Bros, 1904.

Teacup in a Storm

Marie Chanel as Deborah in the 2016 The Q/Joan Sutherland Performing Arts Centre production of Teacup in a Storm *at the Joan Sutherland Performing Arts Centre, Sydney. (Photo: Katy Green Loughrey)*

Teacup in a Storm was first produced by The Q/Joan Sutherland Performing Arts Centre at the Joan Sutherland Performing Arts Centre, Sydney, on 25 February 2016, with the following cast:

    Performer / Interviewer   Therese Cook
    Performer   Marie Chanel

Director, Nick Atkins
Designer, Jonathan Hindmarsh
Sound Designer, Danielle O'Keefe
Lighting Designer, Liam O'Keefe
Production Manager, Geoff Turner
Operator, Ben Turner
Production Support, Ben Turner and Todd Hawken

CHARACTERS/VOICES

In *Teacup in a Storm*'s first production two actors played all the roles. The play, however, lends itself to a larger cast production and features a majority of female roles. Feel free to cast in favour of cultural diversity.

DEBORAH (THE UGLY SISTER) *
LINDSEY
KELLIE
HANNAH'S GRANDDAUGHTER (JANINA) *
ROSIE *
ERIKA
MAUREEN
ANNE
PATRICK
SARA
YVONNE

MULTIPLE OTHER VOICES *

* are fictional characters or voices.

PRODUCTION NOTES

This script is essentially the spoken text of *Teacup in a Storm*. Movement, gesture, sound and visuals are only partially included. Stage directions are suggestions and possibilities rather than absolutes.

Teacup in a Storm blends fictional material with the words of actual carers. The quotes in the documentary portraits (Lindsey, Kellie, Erika, Maureen, Anne and Patrick, Sara and Yvonne) are taken from long interviews. They have been tidied up and sometimes re-ordered, but are basically unedited. All names and other identifying details have been changed.

The script uses punctuation and layout to suggest delivery.

▼ ▼ ▼ ▼ ▼ indicates a change of scene.

ACT ONE

YVONNE *loads laundry from a bucket into a washing machine. At the bottom of the bucket she finds a toddler's yellow knitted sweater. She holds the precious garment. The tiny sweater is illuminated by a light inside the bucket.*

YVONNE *returns it to the bucket and switches off the light.*

Glitter. Spangles. Garish lighting.

Deborah's 'The Ugly Sister' is a framing narrative written as a connected series of late-night, sometimes serious, often blackly comic, monologues.

DEBORAH (THE UGLY SISTER):

This one hot summer day, we all went to Aunty Rachel's for a barbeque: Mum and Dad, my older brother Sam, me and my baby sister Ruth. And Ruth started crying as soon as we got there. For no obvious reason. And the crying became screaming. And the screaming escalated. Mum tried to comfort her, but Ruth kept pushing her away. And screaming louder than ever. Then Mum got upset because she couldn't soothe her, and had no idea what was wrong.

It was the first time I saw my mother cry—but it wasn't the last.

Even then, at the age of seven or eight, I knew that the other grown-ups were looking on and making their own judgments.

What I didn't understand was that our lives—mine and Sam's and our parents'—would never be the same again.

Because of Ruth.

My ugly sister.

I resented Ruth, because until she came along and wrecked everything, *I* was Cinderella in a sparkly dress.

Needy, greedy Ruth sucked up time and energy. There was nothing left over for me and Sam.

When I was fourteen I bought a lock, borrowed tools, and fitted it to my bedroom door. I was fed up coming home from school to find that Ruth had messed up my clothes, destroyed my science project or ripped posters off the walls.

Mum and Dad refused point blank to secure her room with a deadbolt.

'She's your sister. Not a wild animal.'

So I turned the key and retreated to my own safe haven away from the chaos.

Left home to get away from it as soon as I could. I was sick to death of fucking autism.

▼ ▼ ▼ ▼ ▼

A waiting room.

In the following scene the lines are unattributed, but designed for two or more voices.

Magazine?

Magazine?

No thanks.

Sure?

Wouldn't mind a cup of tea—

There's a machine for that.

Right.

Wait for tests.

Wait for more tests.

Next.

Can. You. Make. A. Cup. Of. Tea?

Next.

Can. You. Draw. The. Hands. On. A. Clock?

Wait for results.

Excuse me—?

There's a three- to six-month wait.

That's a long time.

Shall I put you on the list?

LINDSEY:

I care for my twenty-three-year-old daughter who has quite a severe anxiety disorder but to the point where it's crippling … she very rarely leaves the house and when she does it's with great difficulty.

When I'm feeling good I see it as a journey … but on a bad day … [*after a laugh*] on a bad day I hate the world and I want to kill everyone in it.

I didn't think I'd be still looking after my twenty-three-year-old daughter at home like a two-year-old … I did think that by now she would have been independent, that there might be grandchildren … But it's been a gradual loss. I started off thinking she was going to be dux of the school, and now my hope is if she could get a little job in a shop like Woolworths by the time she's thirty …

I've learnt how to shift my values too, and not see success in terms of how society measures success …

If she can't sleep she gets into a panic and that quickly escalates into a psychotic rage where she will scream at me, at the world in general … and there have been occasions where I've had to call the police or ambulance, or the neighbours have called the police because there's such a racket.

When she sleeps late, that's my time to myself, so I often have two hours in the morning, that's my time. While I'm washing up, doing the washing, cleaning up a bit … I enjoy that part of the day because I do have it to myself.

Watching your child suffering, that's probably the hardest part of it. But then to be met with callousness, especially on the part of people who are supposed to be those caring for my daughter … people who are being paid to care but couldn't care less.

Without the disability … we would be different people. And she is more than just her disability too … But if I had a magic wand that could take her disability away, yes, I would take it away in an instant, but … leave the lessons that have been learnt.

When she's good, she's very, very good—but when she is not she is horrid. And when she's good and in a stable mood she's actually quite good company. I like her and I enjoy her company and I think it's very, very sad that none of the rest of the world gets to see what she has to offer it.

On a really bad day I do think perhaps I shouldn't have had children … so I do think, God, if I just hadn't had her I'd have money, time, health, freedom—But, but, but I do think I would have missed out on a huge part of life. That's on a good day.

Some would think I'm an idiot ... some would think I'm a saint.

In the following scene the lines are unattributed, but designed for two or more voices.

Old Mother Hubbard lived in a cupboard—

No. No, she didn't. It just felt like that.

Into the woods and out of the woods and happily ever after—

I don't think so.

They all lived happily ever after.

No, they didn't. You've skipped the middle bit where life gets really difficult and complicated.

Rapunzel was a beautiful baby. But when she turned two an evil witch locked her up. In a high tower where no-one could reach her.

Hi, I'm calling about getting some support for my two-year-old daughter, who has a preliminary diagnosis of—

[*Interrupting*] The person who deals with that won't be in till next Monday. I'll take your details and they'll get back to you as soon as they can.

When do you think that might be?

As soon as they can.

Just when Rapunzel has got used to her isolation—more or less.

Stopped expecting to be rescued.

Along comes the prince with absolutely no idea of her day-to-day reality. Not a clue.

Hang on, we'll get you out of there!

he shouts. Like a television fireman.

When she explains her plight—the evil witch inside, et cetera, and how trapped she is by domestic chores and all that crap she has to comb through—

Hi, can I talk to someone about maybe getting a cleaner?

It's a familiar story, isn't it?

No—well, yes. Sort of.

Don't you have a friend or neighbour who can help you out?

It makes me feel small
As a fingernail or a dust-bunny.
The house is a state, but I can't summon the energy to vacuum.
I just stare at the TV
Pour vodka into a dirty mug.
I know I should have a shower and tidy up—
Instead I'm getting pissed and watching reality shows
'Survivor'—bamboo huts and bickering. Here's an idea: Why don't they put the castaways to work as care-givers and see how they survive?

▼ ▼ ▼ ▼ ▼

KELLIE:

I care for my twin boys. They're autistic and have developmental delays as well ... They were about three when they were diagnosed. I was living in a women's refuge and they asked me if I had any concerns about the boys' development, because we'd come out of, like, domestic violence and all of that, and there was a few red flags ...

I was like having to make up excuses for their behaviour to everyone. But when I learnt that they were autistic it sort of made sense ... the fact that I knew something was wrong, and then they told me something was wrong—so it wasn't anything that I'd done. It was just the way they were. To accept the way they were and try to get other people to accept that that's just the way they are.

I don't feel like I'm part of the normal mum crowd ... And the kids get set apart, like when the boys were at mainstream school, you'd see the other kids getting party invitations and things, and no-one would ever invite the boys because it was too much work for them at their kids' party.

For a lot of years I felt a lot of grief that I'd lost something, like lost the kids that, you know, you expected to have ... Yeah, it is a loss—but there's a gain though ... they're not your normal, average, run-of-the-mill kids. All the things that make them so special, just make them so brilliant.

We tried like different communication systems. Even ones that cost like three hundred dollars and came highly recommended by certain professional people did absolutely nothing ... not one particular thing works, and not one particular thing fails. Like I said, there's no plan, just every day something might change.

I'm doing the best I can. You come and stand in my shoes for an hour and see how you go.

I feel blessed because I know a lot of special needs kids aren't happy. The fact that my boys are happy makes me think that I'm doing something right because they are happy. They might not speak the best or be able to get dressed by themselves, but they're happy.

Sometimes you don't even know yourself because you're so wrapped up in everyone else's needs … you forget about yourself and forget who you are …

The experts kept saying that they're not capable of loving and empathy and all that … Get to know them. They're amazing.

▼ ▼ ▼ ▼ ▼

Again a waiting room.

As before, the lines are unattributed, but designed for two or more voices.

You can't access services until you have a diagnosis.

How long—?

Hard to say. Can't make any promises.

Magazine?

No thanks.

What's the time?

Take a seat.

Wait in line.

Thirteen across, seven letters.

We're both waiting—

Have you been here long?

She shows me how to fill the time with crossword puzzles—

Thirteen across, seven letters. To eat or devour?

Wolf?

Overwhelm?

Consume! C–O–N—

Wait your turn.

Sit tight.

Count to ten.

What's the time?

Take a number.

Wait in line.

We can put him on a waiting list for a special needs playgroup.

How long do you think—?

Next.

Not too long—

Maybe only a few months.

What would really help is a weekly cleaner. Is there a waiting list for that?

No.

How about fortnightly?

We don't do cleaners. But we can offer you two hours of respite care.

A week?

A month.

▼ ▼ ▼ ▼ ▼

Glitter. Spangles. Wine.

DEBORAH (THE UGLY SISTER):

When our parents died, Sam took over caring for Ruth. He wasn't a martyr, he was a journalist—worked a lot from home, so the arrangement worked for him. Sure, I felt guilty about leaving him to cope with her, but I had my marriage and my career was at a critical stage. By the time the marriage folded I'd convinced myself that Sam didn't need my help. He and Ruth were a team … I suppose in a funny sort of way I was jealous of their special relationship.

Then last year Sam was killed in a traffic accident.

And I'm just taking in that awful news when next thing I know Ruth is on my doorstep with this social worker, who seems to think she can off-load the caring role onto me.

No way, I tell her. No way am I up for this. I've had enough of autism. I just want a normal life.

I told the social worker and the people at the day-care centre Ruth goes to that her living with me was only temporary. Until I find a residential home to take her. That I can afford, that doesn't reek of incontinence and cabbage.

If there's anything we can do ... The offers tail off.

Meanwhile I did short courses about how to navigate the disability care system. Went to seminars with experts advocating this or that behavioural technique. Professors reeling off lists of medications that might have been varieties of tomato for all the meaning they had for me.

And I spoke with other carers. But their stories scared the shit out of me. One couple told me that in sixteen years they'd never left their son with anyone else.

What do you do if you want to go out?

'We don't,' they said. 'We haven't been out together since he was born.'

I didn't know what to say. It seemed like a life sentence.

Back to the waiting room and more of the waiting game.

As before, the lines are unattributed, but designed for two or more voices.

Four down, eleven letters—something, something, U.

Feeling blocked. Upset or annoyed by inability to do something.

Ends with N.

[*Counting the letters on her fingers*] F–R–U–S–T—

Did someone mention tea?

Frustration.

Any chance I could get a cup of tea?

There's a waiting period.

Down the corridor.

Wait for blood tests.

Wait and see.

Wait for more tests.

Wait for an appointment with the specialist.

Wait on a plastic chair until your bones ache and your bum goes numb.

Wait until the words are boiling inside you.

▼ ▼ ▼ ▼ ▼

HANNAH'S GRANDDAUGHTER (JANINA):

Hannah stands by the kettle, looking at the kettle, and says, Help me, where's the kettle? Help me. Although not in so many words.

I say, Babcia—that's Nanna in Polish—let me make you a cup of tea.

She says, Ah hah, but I do the crossword and I've still got my knitting. I'm making a sweater for what's-his-name. And not only the cryptic ones with shipshape answers.

I appreciate your straight talk, Babcia—about putting a seat in the shower cubicle, your concern about my future.

We know where we are.

Hannah says, The nurse told me I should hold on to the furniture.

Let me make you that cup of tea. Let me run to the shops and buy us gingerbread and a cake so delicious we'll want to dance with it.

Hannah looks over her shoulder, and says, Have you seen my knitting? It was there on the chair and now it's not. I'm making a scarf for what's-his-name. Such a lovely boy. He lives on Bielańska Street.

Her mother tongue clings to the roof of her mouth.

When she knits, the needles move as if her hands remember of their own accord.

I say, Tell me about Bielańska Street and the people who lived there. The pattern of light on the pavement. Did moss grow between the stones?

Then she says, Don't you ever want to go to the flea market and get lost in dispossessed dresses and someone else's shoes? Don't you want to experiment with silence, ride out in starlight, or catch the slow train to Kraków just for the fun of it?

Then I say, Babcia, shall I make us a cup of tea?

Hannah stands beside a tangle of red and blue knitting wool, looking at the knitting, and says, Where's my knitting? I'm making socks for what's-his-name? The boy from Bielańska Street. We go to the same school but he's in a different class. Have you seen my knitting? Help me, I can't find it …

I say, The lattices and constellations unravelling in your brain have hidden it from you. Let's have a cup of tea, and then I'll help you look for it.

▼ ▼ ▼ ▼ ▼

In the waiting room again.
Unattributed lines for two or more voices.

We can refer you to another agency.

And another waiting list?

We need the documentation before we can address specific needs.
This usually takes about three months.

There's a waiting period for those services?

That's correct.

What about the private sector?

They've got waiting lists as well. But shorter ones.

Excuse me, I thought I was next.

I can't wait anymore.

I could murder a cup of tea.

I was told to be here at ten o'clock, and it's now gone eleven.

Will I lose my place in the queue if I nip to the bathroom?

Excuse me—?

You'll just have to wait.

Magazine?

I make allowances, try to be polite,
Smile in all the right places,
Take hospital corners in my stride—
But it's not easy.

The bad is still happening—

I'm kicked and bitten and bashed. If I tell you it's an abusive spouse there's a bucketload of sympathy and advice. If I tell you the bruises are from my child's punch-happy fists …

Silence.

▼ ▼ ▼ ▼ ▼

Glitter. Spangles. Wine.

DEBORAH (THE UGLY SISTER):

If one more person tells me how wonderful Sam was with Ruth, I'll strangle them with my bare hands.

I just want to get on with my life. Is that so unreasonable? Last year I had a job, friends, a sex life. I did all the things regular, independent adults do. I worked late if I wanted to, went away for weekends, ate what I liked, saw who I liked. There's bugger-all opportunity for any kind of relationship with Ruth around. She's been living with me less than six months and I've become a social pariah.

I can't do this.

I know I should, but I can't.

And if that makes *me* the ugly sister—well, so be it.

She knocks over or drops her wine glass. It shatters.

END OF ACT ONE

ACT TWO

Moths. Keys. Roses.

DEBORAH (THE UGLY SISTER) *sweeps up the broken glass.*

ROSIE:

There's a crash—

It wakes me up.

The phone rings.

It's William, my husband—calling me from the bathroom. He's lost.

He gets lost in familiar places, puts his iPad in the microwave.

He's restless, wants to drive, keeps asking for the car keys.

She reels off a list of excuses.

The car's at the mechanic's, darling.

Someone's borrowed it.

Flat tyre. Flat battery.

It's run out of petrol.

I dropped my bag and the keys fell down the drain.

Hide the car keys.

Lock the door.

It's hard to find the beginning of dementia.

I remember an evening about six years ago. Will had gone to a conference in New Zealand and I was talking to him via Skype.

It was a Saturday, the air tangy with autumn.

One moment we were laughing about university catering, sandwiches filled with grated carrot and mystery meat,

the next I heard his syntax go haywire.

He'd start a sentence about his fellow entomologists, lose his way, and start another.

It scared me, this floundering—

It made me merciless.

I'd wait on the edge of conversations, watch my husband the science professor thrash about for cues, and refuse to help.

That Saturday evening the Skype minutes ticked on.

Outside the clouds churned.

Well, I won't keep you,' he said with sudden desperate cheer like an explorer sighting land. 'I'll say goodnight now.

Bye, darling.

Don't hide behind words. What will happen? How and when? Plain words. I need to know this.

The doctor nodded. And he told me what to expect.

My sister-in-law flew in from England, took one look at the situation and flew back home.

I was on my own.

It's okay, I told Will. We don't need anyone. But of course I did—do. Dear God, do we need help.

Hide the car keys.

Lock the door.

[*Reading, struggling with the Latin and technical terms*] '*Epiphyas postvittana*, the light brown apple moth, is a polyphagous species native to Australia. It has established in New Zealand, Hawaii, Ireland, New Caledonia, Great Britain and California, where it causes widespread damage to pome, citrus and vine crops ...'

On days of muddle, when Will gets agitated, I discovered the quickest way to settle him is by reading aloud his research papers.

[*Reading, as before*] 'Larvae are not easily distinguished from the larvae of other tortricid leafrollers. DNA testing is the only certain method of identification …'

Hide the car keys.

Lock the door.

In the kitchen I tear apart

bread rolls. Put out olives and cheese—a crumbly Wensleydale, Will's favourite.

Darling, let's have lunch in the garden.

The wild roses are still in flower, a veil of bees hovering over them.

What I do must be done each day, every season,

like a liturgy.

Gather up laundry. Check pockets.

Switch on washing machine.

Cycle ends. Tip damp clothes into basket.

Then head outside, singing this hymn I remember from school assemblies:

> [*Singing*] Through the night of doubt and sorrow,
> Onward goes the pilgrim band,
> Singing songs of expectation,
> Marching to the Promised Land.
> And before us, through the darkness …

▼ ▼ ▼ ▼ ▼

The art of translation.

In the following scene the lines are unattributed and designed for two voices.

We want the disabled dollar to work harder.

Translation: We want *you* to work harder—and for less money.

There's been an emphasis on data gathering and capacity building.

Translation: We've generated a lot of paperwork and pie charts.

We don't discriminate. We don't care where you come from, only where you're going.

Ideally as far away from here as possible. Out of sight, out of mind.

We serve a mixed ecology with a range of expertly designed programs.

We know sod-all about the nature of your everyday life.

Alternative translation: We're a lucky dip.

ERIKA:

We have a little four-year-old girl, Cayleigh. We got her when she was eight months old because her birth mother wasn't able to look after her … She was the fifth of five children and the other children were all in care as well …

There's lot of things that we need to do that we wouldn't need to do for our biological child. Like if she has to have surgery or anything it has to be approved by the Department … we have to have stuff approved all the time … I work around these things now … this is the system … so I don't rail against it, I work within the confines. The most challenging thing has been the contact with birth parents …

The bureaucracy is really, really good at never telling you lies, but never telling you all of the facts.

When you first take a child, you think she's long-term, so you're pretty sure that there's really very little chance that she would go back to her birth mother, but you know, there's always that possibility ... Is somebody going to knock on my door one day and just say: Oh, pack Cayleigh up, she's got to go?

I have no rights. I'm not her guardian ... and that's really scary because ... I love Cayleigh more than anything but there's a big risk in there ... But on the other hand, also realising that you can make a difference ... this is one child and I've changed her life and that's huge ... You've got to think about the positives as well.

We became foster parents for our—well, partly selfish reasons, because we wanted another child, but partly unselfish, because we felt there were children in our community that needed homes ... Initially in those first few months it was quite scary: Can I do this? Then you find that you love this child. Biology's got nothing to do with it.

▼ ▼ ▼ ▼ ▼

MAUREEN:

I didn't think of it as a chore ... I wanted him to have the best possible care and to know that he was loved ... It was what I wanted to do.

Hardest thing was seeing him stripped of his ability to do things, the simplest things ... You had to go into the shower with him and get it ready. The soap's there. The towel is here. Show him how to turn things on and everything.

I organised things so that it was easier for them living when I wasn't there ... Early on, my role was like a troubleshooter ... Once breakfast was done and cleaned up, I'd make phones calls. I'd get those done at the start of the day. Then I'd usually try to go out for a walk with Dad.

What would have helped me? Well, living in an extended family where there were aunts and uncles and children, and everyone was doing the caring role. In our culture it's hard to get support—enough support. Because it takes more than one person to care—it takes more than two or three people ...

As the Alzheimer's progressed, we'd just sit together and often there wasn't a lot of talking. We'd go through photo albums ... Nothing matters really more than the connection, and the sitting, and just having time. It doesn't matter if the dishes don't get done.

Glitter. Spangles. More wine.

DEBORAH (THE UGLY SISTER):

After months terrified for Ruth, terrified for myself, feeling helpless, depressed—suicidal—I got her into a residential hostel. Yay!

I went back to work full-time. Started dating someone, my life was almost back on track—when I got a call.

What's happened?

Ruth and some of the other clients were in the garden. The hostel was short-staffed that day, so the clients—quote, unquote—'were left on their own a while'. Ruth must have wanted the toilet, but instead of telling someone, she just did it there and then. Trouble is, the neighbour's grandkids were playing in their backyard and saw Ruth's bare bum through the fence. They've lodged a complaint with the cops: indecent exposure.

We wondered if you'd mind taking her home for a few days until the fuss dies down.

Then she can go back?

Well ... Long pause. We'll have to see. We're trying to persuade the neighbours not to go to the media.

This is lousy timing for me, I told the hostel worker. Feeling like a selfish shit, of course.

We're sorry for the inconvenience, but ...
Yeah, yeah, yeah.

The thought of Ruth living with me on a permanent basis sent me into panic mode. How dare she? How dare she do this to *me*?

It's ridiculous. So she pissed in the bushes. Get over it. Men do it all the time. It's just political.

Look. Deep breath. I'm sure once things calm down ...

But what if they don't? And the next time? What if she does something else that can be misinterpreted? Her behaviour is like that all the time. That's Ruth.

I could be stoic and self-sacrificing and go, 'This is it, the hand I've been dealt, I have to make the best of it.' But when I try to do that, another little voice in my head explodes, 'Fuck it! What have *I* ever done to deserve this?'

▼ ▼ ▼ ▼ ▼

The art of translation again.

As before, the lines are designed for two voices.

We believe in consultation and a better deal for the disabled and their carers.

Translation: The purse is empty.

Moving forward, we're looking to identify strategic need in consultation with portfolio directors and stakeholders.

The purse is empty.

The new programs will transform current services and processes through continuous improvement.

The purse is still empty.

ANNE:

I've got Tyson who is about to turn four, then I've got Jake who is fourteen, and Pia who is nine nearly ten. But my partner Bella and I have also got two biological children ... We also have—Tyson's biological mother has joined our family, and she's the same age as our son, so she's only just turned twenty-one. We have an amazing relationship with her, we really do. It's awesome.

PATRICK:

I've got Luke and he's ten, turning eleven ... I'd come out of a relationship and I decided—I was living on my own and I was working on a magazine and found out that as a gay man I could be a foster carer, which I didn't know ... but it was something that I've always wanted to do ...

I can't imagine my life now without him in it. Everything's changed. How I look at the world ... It's challenging, I admit that ... I'm facing challenges that I never thought I would ever. But I wouldn't have it any other way. People say that he's a very lucky boy to have found me. I say I think I'm a very lucky man that I found him.

ANNE:

Sometimes you don't know what's going to make your life more complete until you actually get it ... As much as you don't want to compare kids to shoes, it's like a pair of shoes that you really, really want and you love them, but they give you blisters. Until you wear them in and until they become comfortable. The blisters come with the shoes and they could be my favourite shoes, but you're going to get blisters.

PATRICK:

He started by calling me *the* carer, then it was *his* carer ... But he acknowledges me now as his dad and that's what I am ... We're the ones who stay up with them. We soothe their fears. We look after them when they're sick. We share in their joys and gloomy days—we *are* their parents.

ANNE:

There are always those people who are your friends who don't understand why you would do this ... You could start travelling the world, you could do whatever you wanted, you had a big social life ... There's also people who can't understand the kids' behaviour ... So, yeah, we did lose a lot of friends along the way ... But I've gained so much. Far more than I've lost.

PATRICK:

If there's a crisis, yes, we do have to notify the agency, but we notify each other and then we come in and we support each other ... Agencies don't do that.

ANNE:

People are always curious. The first thing they want to know is why the children are in care ... and then you have to deal with that because it isn't any of their business ... Sometimes well-meaning people will become dithering idiots who go, Oh, it's so terrible. I couldn't do what you do. Really! I really don't need to know that. Don't turn me into Mother Theresa ... We're not saints. We're just people with a capacity to love.

PATRICK:

I think in the gay community I'm seen as something of an oddity. Why would you do that? Why would you give everything up for a child? ... As a single male, I think a lot of people look at me and say, What's wrong with you? Why are you doing that?

ANNE:

There's a prejudice against gay parents. There's a prejudice against foster children because there's always got to be a story, and that's what people want to know. They want to make a story.

They want to make a story.

They want to make a story.

In the following scene the lines are unattributed, designed for two or more voices.

Once upon a time there was a couple who had been wishing for a child. For such a long time ...

Did you know—?

What?

In the original versions of Snow White and Hansel and Gretel it was their biological mother not the wicked stepmother who sent them into the forest to die.

    Beat.

Once ever after—

Why do it?

Do what?

Why look after a child that's not related to you? And with special needs. Is it the money?

[*After a laugh*] As if!

Is it a religious thing?

What's that African saying about children being a communal responsibility?

It takes a village to raise a child.

> *Beat.*

Once ever after there were a king and queen who couldn't have children, but desperately wanted them—

Birth parents have rights. That's the law.

I know.

Then one day—

You're asking for trouble.

One day while the queen was bathing, a crab crawled out of the water and said: Your wish will be granted—

You hear such horror stories, don't you?

Millions of people have kids. They don't necessarily have them in perfect circumstances.

Yeah, that's true, but still …

Less than a year later, the queen had a daughter—

Problem kids are problem kids.

They're kids *dealing* with problems, not problem kids. Big difference.

What if you're so flat out with all the fostering stuff and fallout from contact visits, you've got no time for your own children? And *they* go off the rails?

The king wanted to protect their daughter—

How does she get on with your other kids?

Like all siblings.

They compete. For attention, pocket money, time on the computer, the last jelly snake in the packet.

But why a child with *extra* needs?

Why not? Her life is just as valuable as any neurotypical.

What's neurotypical?

Someone who's not on the autism spectrum or been diagnosed with an intellectual or developmental disability.

    Beat.

While the girl was asleep she was raped by her father, and—still comatose   gave birth to twins. One of the babies sucked her finger which removed the splinter that was keeping her asleep.

That's the original Sleeping Beauty story.

Pity the teenager who wakes up to find herself mother of two kids.

Those stories are everywhere.

Everywhere and invisible at the same time.

For ever and never.

The girl will eat an apple, pick a rose. One way or another she will bleed, scream and get entangled in the foster system.

Glitter and spangles now not so bright and shiny. Wine.

DEBORAH (THE UGLY SISTER):

Ladies and gentlemen!

There's Ruth in the living room with the TV way too loud. And here's me on my hands and knees scrubbing the kitchen floor.

Why the Cinderella act? Because the orange juice was in the wrong type of carton. Not the ones they had at the hostel.

Ruth took exception to the change and chucked it all over the place.

Thing is, I never really know why she has these blow outs. Could be the different carton, could be something on TV, could be the bloody weather for all I know, but whatever it is, it upsets her. Lucky this time it's juice. [*After a laugh*] We'll be sticking to the tiles for weeks, but nothing broken. Last outburst she smashed the coffee table.

Smash! The sound of furniture being broken.

▼ ▼ ▼ ▼ ▼

Moths. Keys. Roses.

ROSIE:

There's a crash—

The phone rings.

It wakes me up.

It's my husband …

I'm holding on to a takeaway coffee.

I'm holding on to hope.

Nurses murmur.

Lights flicker.

I'm cursing myself for leaving the keys where he could find them. For not waking up in time to stop him.

Relieved the accident involved no other vehicle, no-one else is hurt.

Nurses murmur.

Lights flicker.

Eleven thousand miles away, his mother and sister wait for my call.

'Mrs Kavanagh—Rosie?'

Someone calls my name.

The doctor says my husband

does not have—my husband will live

is the answer.

His injuries will impact mobility, his walking, he may need a wheelchair, she says—but there's something else …

And then she tells me what I already know, what we've been dealing with for several years: early-onset Alzheimer's.

I go in to see him.

Will used to be a big man, over six feet in the old money,

but he's shrunk—

All except the hands. Look at them! [*With a laugh*] 'Big as boots,' he jokes.

As I'm leaving the hospital—

WOMAN IN HOSPITAL:

Rosie!

ROSIE:

Out of the blue, a woman I've never met gives me a bunch of roses.

I overheard the doctor call your name,' she says. 'I've been where you are.

Hide the car keys.

Lock the door.

Put your arms around my neck—
And wrap him close.
There we go—
I hear the frog in his throat
when he tries to tell me what he's done,
talks about his past life in science,
or the whole shitstorm of medication and loss.

Put your arms around my neck—
And lift him up.
There we go—
From the armchair to the wheelchair.
My back hurts but I don't let on
that I can see stars trembling in his sweat,
that he feels cold to the touch.

We are good and strange to one another.
On the table among a library of appointment cards
for clinics and specialists,
a Kodak snapshot on an English seafront:
wedding-day William and Rosie—
And Siouxsie and the Banshees' 'Helter Skelter'.

>   *She laughs.*

Will's family couldn't believe we'd chosen that song.
They were thinking something churchy or romantic,
but it wasn't us. We did it with spiky hair and punk.

>   *Beat.*

We think we know ourselves, but all we know is: love surprises us.

Beat.

Friends and former colleagues visit with bakestuffs,
bring sweetness to the door,
breaking news from the insect world—
How are you feeling? If you need a hand …

Put your arms around my neck—
And hold tight.
Are you sure, darling? It's started raining—
Oh, what the hell.

The pop of a champagne cork.

Let's crack open the champagne.
Let's watch the fireworks out-rage the storm.
Let's anniversary in style!
Put your arms around my neck—
And let me remember the last time I was held by a lover …

Music. Something raw and punk circa late 1970s.

The storm that's been brewing now breaks with lightning and the crash of thunder.

END OF ACT TWO

ACT THREE

SARA:

You just cope, cope, cope, cope, cope, and then you fall apart and then pick yourself up and you cope, cope, cope.

It's not a disability that you can see when you look at a person, but the behaviours are very challenging, being very overwhelming … you're educating people all the time … and it's exhausting, it's exhausting … the having to always keep explaining.

There's always the question: How much have you got in the bucket to deal with what's about to come your way?

▼ ▼ ▼ ▼ ▼

In the following scene the lines are unattributed, and designed for two or more voices.

If you were a fairytale character, who would you be?

Sleeping Beauty. Imagine all that uninterrupted sleep.

The stories are there—if you listen.

Once upon a time there was a woman who longed for a child of her own.

I'm sensing a bit of a theme here.

She had no idea how to get one, so off she went to—

Family and Community Services?

No. To an old witch. Who gave her a grain of barley.
Plant it in a flowerpot and watch what happens.

It's a miracle!

The seed grows and blossoms into a minute, thumb-size girl. The woman calls her daughter Thumbelina.

You can't fix your child like a broken saucer.

The tiny girl falls prey to a lascivious beetle, and a—

[*Interrupting*] Pick on someone your own size.
It's a constant fight.

I'm up at the school.
Again.
They mean well.
The teacher explains their aim is to make Tom happy and comfortable. That's lovely, I say, but he needs more. He needs to be pushed to do things for himself.
'He's got support from an assistant …'
'Yes, but that separates Tom from his classmates. Leaves him stranded in the computer room with an assistant four times his age.'

Once upon another time there was the princess and the pea.

That's P–E–A, not pee as in piss.

There's a prince—

There's always a prince.

And this prince wants to marry a princess, but he's having trouble finding one. Then one foul and stormy night a young woman knocks on the front door—

Of the castle?

Yes. She's freaked out by the wild weather, totally lost the plot, claiming to be a princess. The prince's mother takes stock of the situation—

Offers the girl a bed for the night?

In the bed she puts a pea—

P–E–A.

And covers it with a stack of mattresses and feather quilts.

The young woman climbs up the padded mountain and lies down.

But she can't sleep.

She tosses and turns.

Instead of sweet dreams she flies into a major panic—

[*Interrupting*] Because of the pea in her bed which has to be made just so.

The next morning and most mornings I'm changing piss-soaked sheets. No magic wand, no three wishes come true. No kiss and make it better. The frog stays a frog. One thousand and one nights of sheer hell with no fairy godmother on the horizon. The pumpkin is just a vegetable, nothing magical about it.

Nothing magic at all.

If you were a fairytale character, who would you be?

Sleeping Beauty. Not for the prince. For all that continuous sleep.

Well, smash me, looking glass.

Nights are gruelling. Eight o'clock becomes nine becomes midnight, and I'm still trying to get him settled. Rock-a-bye baby. Time for sleeping, sweetheart. Finally he drops off and I tiptoe to my own room. My head touches the pillow and I'm dead to the world—for an hour, two if I'm lucky. Before he climbs out of bed, and I put him back. [*She yawns.*] Night, night, sweetie. Sleep tight. Again. By four I'm dog tired and all I can think of is that in two hours [*yawning again*] I have to get up and catch a train to be at work for a nine-thirty meeting.

Naturally it's your own decision, but—

But.

Always a but. Just when it looks as if my life is back within grasp, something swings by to knock it out again.

It's great that you're taking on the caring.

There wasn't much choice.

No. There isn't for any of us.

Finding out that Tom is—is, let's say 'different'—was a lonely experience. Until one day, by total coincidence, I met Thumbelina's mother in the doctor's waiting room.

A moment of recognition. Connection.

We grieved for the son and daughter we didn't have, and never would.

It never stops.

Every time your child fails to reach another milestone you grieve all over again. For what might have been. One of the hardest things is when you realise they're not children anymore. They're adults and they're never going to change. Thumbelina is always going to be the size of a woman's thumb.

▼ ▼ ▼ ▼ ▼

Numbers.

As before, the unattributed lines are designed for two or more voices.

The performers fold and juggle laundry as they swap statistics like you share gossip.

Recipe for a pie chart:

Take a circle. Cut in two. Put aside one half for admin. Divide remaining half into several unequal slices. Stir in some sweeteners. Season to taste.

I woke up this morning

to a morning thick with mist, and

my eyes inflamed, a scratchy throat—

    She coughs.

There's paracetamol for that. I'll expect you in ten.

Being sick isn't an option.

You can't express love in forms and flow charts. That's worry number one.

Who cares?

Two-point-seven million Australians care.

Two-point-seven million people provide care for an elderly person or someone with a disability or long-term health condition.

Who cares?

Seventy per cent of primary carers are women.

A hundred and fifty thousand carers are under the age of fifteen.

Seven-point-three per cent are seventy-five and older.

Do the maths.

Carers provide one-point-nine billion hours of unpaid care.

Save tax payers an estimated forty-point-nine billion dollars per annum.

When you're up to your elbows in a bucket, or changing a colostomy bag, numbers mean nothing. Zero.

Twenty-four divided by one equals twenty-four,
times seven equals a week.
A week times fifty-two equals a year—

Minus a week's respite leaves fifty-one which equals one carer,
plus three kids beyond their mother's call,
two red apples,
and one sock that isn't anywhere you look.

What does it all add up to?

Nine times out of ten.

No two ways about it.

More than fifty per cent of carers experience some measure of depression.

Over a third experience severe or extreme stress.

The kitchen's a battlefield of breakfast and broken china,
burnt miles of toast
you want to scream—

You want to run away—

One, two, three—Breathe.

Five, six—Breathe.

SEVERAL VOICES:
Breathe.

Back to single voices.

Ninety-nine per cent of statistics tell less than half the story.

Do you know?

Statistics say
take a hundred people, and
how many of them always know better than you?

Rough guess somewhere between fifty and sixty.

How many are happy to help—if it doesn't take too long?

Maybe a third.

If it takes longer?

Down to a quarter.

Do you know?

Mental health carers spend on average a hundred and four hours per week caring for their loved ones.

Now it's your turn.

>   *Hands a bucket to* YVONNE.

But—

Over to you.

▼ ▼ ▼ ▼ ▼

YVONNE *holds the little yellow sweater from the beginning of Act One.*

YVONNE:

One autumn nearly a long time ago, I was reading a Sunday newspaper. I noticed an article about two babies needing permanent homes. Both had Down Syndrome and the girl also had heart issues. Michael, my husband, had recently undergone open heart surgery, so we knew our hearts.

Plus we already had two children.

This sounds absurd, but I knew that baby girl was meant to be my daughter.

So began a saga of phone calls, meetings, interviews, more interviews, home visits, final interviews and then … waiting. Until we learnt we'd been chosen to be Baby Amber's new family. That was the name her birth mother gave her—Amber, like the gold of ancient trees.

We were given a small photo. I showed that picture of Amber to everyone, even strangers on the bus.

>   *She laughs.*

We went to meet her at her foster parents' house. It was a strange and beautiful moment the first time I held my unknown daughter.

She was seven months old when we finally brought her home.

I was over the moon.

The neighbourhood children baked her a welcome cake with pink icing.

The memory brings a smile.

I know this sounds like a fairy story—

ANOTHER VOICE:

But it's a true story, isn't it?

It's *your* story.

Beat.

YVONNE:

Why did we do it?

Michael and I were both registered nurses. We'd worked in institutions. That experience affected us deeply.

I became a carer through the definition of others. Institutions and systems gave me that label, and I adopted it in order to access the necessary support. But when I looked after my children with additional needs I identified as Mother, Mum or Mummy. I still do.

I don't know what label should be used ... but I don't think the same word should refer to people who get paid a wage to care and leave at the end of their shift.

Has being a carer changed me? Of course it has. It's hardened and softened and stretched my heart. Smashed it into a thousand jagged pieces—but then knitted it back together. Sometimes I'm scared it'll wear out, like elastic that's been through the wash cycle too many times. But then I see someone really connect with my daughter, and my heart sings.

What's surprised me?

Pressure from within the disability community to have the so-called genius child. As if you're letting the side down if your child doesn't have a photographic memory for numbers. Isn't a Paralympic athlete or an outgoing personality. A high-achieving ambassador for disability.

And that's on top of pressure from the regular community. To police the aesthetics of your loved one. A regular kid can have a snotty nose or sound off in public, but for a child with a disability—Well! That's just plain offensive.

And don't get me started on the school that thought my daughter's presence would be unfair for the other children. Or the ballet students who literally turned their backs to exclude her.

Anyway—

Amber became Amber-Cate and then Cate. Dreaming her own dreams and dancing to her own tune.

I met her birth mother when Cate was two. I wrote to her. I wanted her to see Cate, and I wanted to take a photo, so my daughter would always have an image of her birth mother. *Her* mum—Cate's biological grandmother—sent two little jumpers she had knitted, one yellow, one white. Cate still has the yellow one.

Rain.

DEBORAH (THE UGLY SISTER):

When I was growing up I never considered what Mum and Dad might be going through with Ruth. I didn't acknowledge their courage or their patience. All I did was complain about my ugly sister and how no-one understood *me*, and if I couldn't go to the ball and wear the glass slippers it wasn't fair.

I never thanked my brother Sam for taking on the responsibility either. He just did it.

And I got on with my life.

The wind got up to gale force tonight, one of those intense summer storms, and Ruth refused to go to sleep. Usual tactics, I sat on her bed for ages, trying to persuade her to stay there. Finally, three-fifteen—success. I stare at her eyelids, pale and tender like mushroom skins, and feel this confusion of love and sorrow and resentment ... but mostly love now she's asleep.

> *She laughs.*

Of course *I'm* now wide awake.

Three-twenty-five I'm in the kitchen filling the kettle.

They've arranged a case conference next week to decide what will happen to Ruth. The hostel's neighbours have made it clear that they don't want her living back there.

The social worker says she's sorry.

Right.

But it isn't right.

I know that and so does the social worker.

Not everything works out how you'd like it to. Sometimes there's no resolution. Sometimes you have to live with that, and it's the hardest thing.

I take my cup of tea to the window and watch the rain hurl itself against the glass.

What am I going to do?

I don't know.

You just do the best you can.

YVONNE:
There's no other way to do it.

THE END

www.ingramcontent.com/pod-product-compliance
Lightning Source LLC
Chambersburg PA
CBHW042131160426
43198CB00022B/2974